GET YOUR
HANDS
OUT OF MY POCKET

*The Hands-On Guide to Helping You
Avoid the Child Support System*

GET YOUR HANDS OUT MY POCKET

OUT MY POCKET

The Hands-On Guide to Avoiding the Child Support System

Authored by

RW Jones

Contributions Made By Charles M. Griffin

RN Spencer
THE BRILLIONAIRE

E-Autograph

Get Your Hands Out My Pockets
Copyright © 2020 by RW Jones. All rights reserved.

No part of this publication may be reproduced, stored in a retrieval system or transmitted in any way by any means, electronic, mechanical, photocopy, recording or otherwise without the prior permission of the author except as provided by USA copyright law.

The opinions expressed by the author are not necessarily those of Can I Live, Inc.

Published by Can I Live, Inc
PO Box 25502 | Alexandria VA 22313 | 202.996.0880 | www.canilive.org

Can I Live, Inc is committed to excellence, accountability and personal responsibility. The company reflects the philosophy established by its founder, based on Proverbs 29:2, "When the Righteous are in Authority, the People Rejoice, But When the Wicked Rule, the People Mourn."

Book design copyright © 2020 by RW Jones. All rights reserved. Book Cover

Design by Elton Benjamin
Researched by Kelvin Spragley
Technical Assistance and Editing by Charles Griffin–Griffin Global Enterprises

Published in the United States of America ISBN: 978-0-9855498-5-5
1. Self-Help / Personal Growth / General
2. Family & Relationships / Parenting / Single Parent

TABLE OF CONTENTS

Preface
Using Data to Change Policy

Background
The Story Behind the Story

Foreword
Vinston Rozier

Introduction
Why this Handbook for Men?

Chapter One
The Relationship — 1

Chapter Two
The Wiring of a Woman — 13

Chapter Three
The Art of Communication — 27

Chapter Four
The Dilemma — 41

Chapter Five
The Catch 22 — 57

Chapter Six
The Do's & Don'ts — 70

Chapter Seven
The Game Plan — 87

Acknowledgments
Father's Forever — 95

Preface
Using Data to Change Policies

Preface

It is important to understand why this book was written. This book advocates for a solution to jailing poor men for nonpayment of child support for the following reasons:

1. Incarcerating men for child support make it impossible for them to support their families in ways that provide a physical presence, financial contribution and keep a source of guidance and information.

2. Though incarceration is designed to be a punishment to correct behaviors, it may exacerbate the inability for poor men to work and pay child support, thus further contribute to non-payment of child support.

3. Men who have trouble paying child support because of lack of education and low income need training to help them be better fathers and help to find gainful employment and specialized jobs skill training.

4. Poor men are jailed without the right to a court appointed attorney. Non-payment of child support is not considered a crime; however men are jailed for being in contempt of court.

An attorney would ensure that child support defendants' rights are protected, their incomes accurately measured, and child support payments fairly set.

As a result of studying the effects of policies to incarcerate men for not paying child support; we discovered that these policies have the effect of incarcerating many poor men who are unable to pay child support. Many of these men would under other conditions pay child support.

The population represented in the research is composed of 56 individuals who currently participate in Father's Forever; a program that trains fathers to take a more active role in their children's lives in addition to fulfilling their financial responsibilities. Father's Forever is a program that substitutes training for incarceration. Its participants are men who were court ordered to participate in the program instead of being sent to jail. Some of these men played active roles in their children's lives and contributed as much as they could financially, yet still faced jail time.

The ages of the participants ranged from 23-55, with the majority dropping out of high school. According to the data, participants had from 1-5 children that they were responsible for and were being challenged by the respective mothers for child support. Of the 56 men who responded to the survey, 40 of them noted that they had been incarcerated before for various reasons. All of them classified themselves as earning low income or unemployed. Through the data collected, we conclude that there is a direct correlation between low income, lack of education, unemployment, the number of children by different mothers, and the father's lack of ability to pay child support.

Data suggests that current policies are unjust as they jail men for their inability to pay debt; a concept that was outlawed by the federal government in 1833. The Department of Justice, the American Bar Association, The Southern Center for Human Rights and The American Civil Liberties Union all argue against the unfair incarceration of men for child support.

Kelvin L. Spragley, Ph.D.
The Spragley Group, LLC
www.spragleygroup.com

Background
The Story Behind The Story

If you're thinking, "Every time I turn around, it's something else holding me back," then I have got to tell you, YOU ARE ABSOLUTELY RIGHT! There will always be trying situations that test your commitment to success. If not handled properly they will keep you from advancing economically and socially. If you are reading this book you may be a young man in his teens or a young father not sure how to handle the pressures of parenthood. Some of you may have realized by now that the child support system is unforgiving. It will chew you up and spit you out if you are not knowledgeable of how to navigate its cold waters.

This handbook will suggest ways in which you can stay out of child support court. If you apply the principles here to your everyday decision-making process, they will help you to become better fathers, establish better relationships with your parent-partners, protect yourself from the child support system, and encourage you to avoid the poor decisions that lead to unplanned pregnancy. This book is for all men–potential fathers and fathers alike, especially working men who would like to save and grow their money into something more meaningful outside of spending their entire income for consumption purposes.

You've heard the saying, "Hell hath no fury like a woman's scorn." Well, that statement is absolutely true. There is nothing like a woman's scorn, and you want to avoid that scorn with every resource you have. This book is designed to help you do just that. By helping you avoid the scorn of your child's mother and her henchmen in the child support system.

If you are not prepared to play the game of life with your "A game", there is a strong possibility that you will lose and this, my brother, is the hard cold truth. The great news is the "A game" is different for every man. No two men will have the same "A game" look and feel. The truth is we are all on different levels and stages in our lives. What is an expected "A game" for the CEO of a top fortune 500 company is much different from a professor at a university and certainly different from a postman or pizza delivery man. The "A game" is in simple terms being what I call "Absolute"! Absolute is being complete, needing nothing–lacking nothing; it cannot be subtracted or added to. It is not mixed with anything for it is pure–it is solid! This is where you want to be. The word "game" is not to be taken literally or lightly. This is not a game. This is real life. You should prepare and play like a champion if you expect to win.

Background: The Story Behind the Story

You must first prepare your heart to want to be the best man that you can be. What does this mean? It is not what a man puts into his mouth that makes him polluted, it is what comes out of his mouth that makes him polluted. Your mouth only utters what is in your heart, so as you can see, the work that needs to be done to push you in the right direction is an internal work. The heart is the core of who we are and what we do. Before you can be a better father or make the decisions that will prevent you from becoming a father before you are ready, your heart must be totally resolved towards accomplishing these goals. When your heart is ready, you will be ready to act and communicate with a spirit of positivity that builds strong healthy relationships and generates desired outcomes.

Your "A game" has nothing to do with games, lies, deceit, ill intentions, selfish ambitions, or motives. It has everything to do with making sure that the principals you hold dear to your heart are Godly principals, and that you are a living example of those principals. This book is about helping you find those principals to help you be the man that God intends for you to be. For those who choose to muddle through life with no sense of purpose or direction, understand that there is a way that seems right unto man, but will surely end in destruction. There will be no other cards for you to shuffle, deal, or play. Your poor decisions will eventually create a bed that you will have to lie in–as difficult as it may be. So why wait, let us try a better way together today!

I want to thank my sons' fathers for giving me the writing material. Who knew that God would turn all the foolishness, chaos, and confusion into something wonderful? They were the motivation behind this book. For twelve years I analyzed and observed every word, action, and behavior from them, so I thank them for leading the way to a creative work that will help bridge the gap and bring light to the systemic lack of fatherhood within the black community and nation as a whole.

If you haven't heard my story, I will give you the short version. Thirteen years ago, I found myself pregnant with a child from a man I thought I would marry. I would tell the man of my dreams almost every day that God either sent him in my life or will use him to benefit me–either way I would win in the end. Needless to say, this man gave me my first son and was a direct connection to the doors of destiny for my life. He worked in a juvenile facility and was able to get me a job working as a youth counselor. It was there that I found the fruit of a problem that I was created to solve. Notice I said the fruit. It has taken me thirteen years of education and thousands of dollars in student loan debt to get to the root of the issue–but that is the subject of another book.

So here I am working in this secure juvenile facility where we had in our care one hundred-sixty (160) young females who were sentenced there for committing some offense. I noticed that out of one hundred-sixty (160) girls, one hundred-fifty-eight (158) of them were African American who lived with a single mom. None knew their dads and they all were high school dropouts. I thought no way was this an accident! My antennas went up and I knew there was something that was going on that was the result of a common, systemic problem in society.

I was compelled and I mean seriously compelled to solve this problem. The first place I decided to go for answers was the classroom. I enrolled in school as a criminal justice major looking to save these young girls. The questions I asked could not be answered on that level and so I knew very early on that this journey would be a very long one. I was enrolled in a local community college as a single mother and having major issues making ends meet. I went to the department of social services for help. They told me I had to come out of school in order for them to help me. They would pay for me to get a CNA (Certified Nurse's Assistant) certificate, but not a criminal justice, political science or law degree. So I did what any woman in her RIGHT mind would have done. I stayed in school and decided that this was the road I would have to take because it was not just about me. I had one hundred-sixty (160) girls to save. Before I could get a full year under my belt, I got pregnant for the second time. I thought okay this was not the plan, but in fact I had no real plan. You have heard people say that if you fail to plan then you plan to fail. Well, I had clearly failed to plan, but I knew for sure that failing was not an option for me. I had to do something to make a change for my future.

In school, struggling as a single mother I thought things could not get any worse until I found myself pregnant again. No way, I thought to myself. I am blaming everyone for my mistakes. I blamed the devil's temptation for my transgressions until one day a pastor of a church said, "It's not the devil, it's you." That was my sobering moment. But not sobering enough until I found myself pregnant again. That's right I said it, pregnant again for the fourth time. It took me five years to complete a two-year degree. I was trying to solve a problem that I was becoming. I was having children out of wedlock. So, I am the woman who knows firsthand about child support, welfare, court, etc.

Since then, I have obtained my Associates in Criminal Justice, Bachelors in Politics, Economics and Law, and a Master's degree in Public Administration. I have started a non-profit called Can I Live, Incorporated. Our mission is to use our knowledge about governance, civic engagement, and public policy to facilitate self-advocacy, community development and opportunity creation for the people and organizations we serve. We are currently working on a Fatherhood Initiative to prevent the incarceration of poor men.

This book and the others that will come are only the beginning of me coming back to save those young girls who are now adult women. The sad part of it all is that most of the youth detention centers, jails and other secure facilities across the United States are filled with Black youth. I believe that it is our duty to do more to make sure that Black youth have the parenting and support they need to be healthy, productive citizens.

I tried very hard to avoid the child support system for the fathers of my children. Instead of involving the court system, I wanted them to take responsibility for their children. I wanted nothing more than for them to have a relationship with their sons. Out of the three men I have children by, one continues to dodge the Sheriff when they come knocking on the door. Can we say trifling? He is an example of what not to be.

So now you have the cliff notes version of how I got to this place. I shared my story with you to let you know that I am here with you in the trenches, in the hustle and grind but on a professional level with a Kingdom flow. The flow is much different on this side; however, I hope to help some of you make that transition.

I want to thank Glen Warren and the men who took the time to read and evaluate this book. Your contributions to this creative work will not go unnoticed. Your honest and open feedback, I believe makes this book a best seller.

I want to dedicate this book to a young man by the name of Fitzgerald Black aka Fred. He is a young father who always watched his children and provided for them at the level in which he was capable. He was recently arrested because he owed about three thousand dollars in child support. His son's mother went down to apply for Social Services and she had to disclose his whereabouts which inherently, per their policies, pursued him for child support. Fred has never been in jail a day of his life and has never committed a crime. He was in jail for over three weeks, until his mother could arrange for him to be placed on house arrest. Fred would watch his son while the mother would go to work and provide pampers, milk, baby food and other necessities, however this was not counted as support. Why? Simply because Fred did not give an accurate account of his support with evidence of having it outlined in a detailed manner. Simply telling the judge obviously was not enough as the judge refused to acknowledge his efforts of support. Now, Fred has a criminal record and although finding employment is not totally impossible, it is much more difficult when you have a criminal record. Even if Fred was working, he would have lost his job after being incarcerated for over three weeks–making it even more difficult to support his child. The fact that Fred was incarcerated, though he was a supportive and caring father, cannot be understated. That is why it is so important for men to know the system, and know what fathers can do to avoid being victimized.

Were you aware that judges interpret the laws and in most states are elected officials voted by the general public? So, my next question to you is... when was the last time you voted for a judge? Judges are probably the least paid attention to name on the ballot; yet have such a significant impact on the lives of those who appear before them in the court room. People run for office to be able to influence policy and make decisions on behalf of others and we vote for people who we believe will do this job to the best of their ability. You should not only pay close attention to all elections, but you should vote for the judge that you believe will best represent you during your next judicial election. If you are not sure when that is, call your board of elections and ask them. Also do not be afraid to call those who are running for office and let them know the issues you are having. Judges can be one of your best advocates if you hold them accountable to the promises they make on the campaign trail.

What will it take for us to take our communities back? It is my hope that this book will contribute to community conversations and solutions that support the rebuilding of the man's role in the family. It is going to take strong men to be the pillars of the family in order to improve the community. The first step in this direction is to help men become more active, more supportive fathers. In order for them to do this they must become better communicators, develop working relationships with their parent partners, seek legal counsel in child support cases, and most importantly follow-up on their passions to become better men–better fathers.

It is my goal to take this work and create systemic change within our communities by offering education and training on; better ways to communicate and understand one another and how policy impacts the very fabric of our everyday lives.

Foreword
by Vinston Rozier

Foreword

Being a good Dad doesn't require money, riches or fame. The fact that you are reading this book shows that you desire to be more to your child than a title. While as a judge I cannot endorse one book over another, I can tell you that this book offers ideas to take you to the next level of fatherhood while navigating your way through the challenges that may come with child support.

The vast majority of parents who have a child support order never come to court. There are typically two reasons for people to come to a Child Support issue: 1) the establishment of a child support payment or 2) a contempt hearing concerning the failure to pay child support. Presiding as a Judge in a Wake County Child Support Courtroom is an experience like none other. As a Judge, there are the positives that come with assisting parents to financially support their children. But this courtroom often reveals the unfortunate negative cycles that occur in the lives of many families.

I have had men come to court and tell me that they see their child every month for the regular trip to McDonald's. Well, they can see the mailman 6 days a week. I hope that something in this book causes you to elevate yourself from a biological father to someone a child can call "dad" and actually have the word mean something that will transcend future generations. As a judge, I can tell you that being this type of father makes a difference in court. I am more likely to give a man a second or third chance when he acts like a "father" than when he simply acts like a donor who now cannot donate money for the fruit of his seed.

To help guide the way through the process of contempt hearings, there are attorneys present in our courtroom to represent those who have not hired attorneys for themselves. These attorneys speak with the Child Support Enforcement Case Workers and attempt to reach a resolution. However, people really need to know what to do before getting into court. So, I am happy that you have decided to read this book to find your path to becoming a better parent and to avoid the traps so many fall into when it comes to child support.

In Child Support Court, I have seen the consequences of children disconnected from their fathers, parents who cannot find work after being incarcerated and developing a criminal record, and too many people who believe they are entitled to state support based upon the grace of their citizenship. There is the evidence of substance abuse, mental and physical disabilities, and joblessness that has been passed from generation to generation. This often reveals itself as the root of problems for so many citizens involved in child support cases.

All the while, it is disappointing how many individuals play by all the proper rules and who diligently struggle, but rarely succeed at making ends meet. These people from all walks of life have dedicated themselves to sacrificing whatever is necessary in order to financially provide for their families. This financial support may come in the form of paying child support. These sacrifices may also be seen by parents doing all that is possible to insure that their child is provided for, regardless of whether the child support owed arrives and arrives on time. So many parents have not subscribed to the selfishness of the "me" culture but are still unable to pay their child support.

Unfortunately, child support cases often come down to issues that have nothing to do with financial support at all. For example:

A. Custody matters are handled separately from child support matters;
B. There have been occasions when a mom will not allow a father to see a child until he pays support or conversely that a father will not pay support unless he is able to see the child on his terms; and
C. There have been times when a father did not want to pay support unless he had a detailed accounting of how the money was being used.

These and other issues that arise often reveal the complexities faced by parents who find themselves in court. However, what is often lost in the discussion is the child for whom the support is to be paid. Too often, these children are from fatherless homes. Seldom, do they interact with their fathers. Frequently, they are exposed to the struggles of unemployed parents. At times, these children learn at early ages about all the details of their parents' troubled relationship and eventually learn to expect the same drama for their own personal futures.

Parents, who appear in court regularly, often need guidance to avoid their regular involvement of the court system in their lives. So, at times, a judge will often choose from options other than jail, house arrest, or probation to move forward. A judge may order or even allow voluntarily attendance in a program established to assist child support defendants in obtaining employment and/or becoming better parents. But still, sitting in a classroom will not make someone a better father or get them a job.

At some point, there is a moment where that person has to make the decision not to give up or to even try. For some, that moment takes place while sitting in a classroom and someone says something that mirrors exactly what they have been experiencing. For others, that moment takes place when a mother refuses to allow a father to have time with his child that he contributed to bringing into the world because of child support. For you, that moment to try or to never give up has already occurred. That is why you have picked up this book. That is why you have taken the time from all the other things that you could otherwise be doing, just to move forward to get out of the rat race you know you are in. I do hope that you are able to gather something from this book to guide you.

Again, being a good dad doesn't require money, riches or fame. The fact that you are reading this book indicates that you desire to be more for your child than a title. The author has offered some ideas to take you to that next level and to navigate your way through the challenges that may come with child support. Learn and move to that higher level.

-Vinston Rozier
Wake County District Court Judge

INTRODUCTION
Why This Handbook For Men?

Introduction: Why This Handbook For Men?

Today's jails are overcrowded and courts are jammed-packed with individuals who have committed nonviolent offenses such as failing to pay child support. If only men knew the secret to staying out of the child support system; if only they knew that most women are not out for their money, but simply need help from the father of their child. I will keep it real and admit that some child support suits are simply about money or vindictiveness. However, for the most part, if a man finds himself in court it is likely due to a poor relationship with his child's mother or because he has been irresponsible. Our goal is to teach you how to create a productive relationship with your parent-partner and encourage you to take more of an active role in raising your children. Doing these two things will make all the difference in the world.

This book's focus is to address the growing number of men backlogging the child support courts with prospective dates to establish paternity and child support. We are at a critical time in history where the lack of fathers in the home is at an all-time high. Though the child support system aims at forcing men to be responsible for their children, it is notorious for treating men unjustly. This book is designed to provide support for men to help them transition to becoming better fathers, and avoid the pitfalls of the child support system.

Our goal is to increase the number of men who are supportive fathers, while decreasing the number of men who are mistreated and incarcerated by the system.

I often tell men that they are losing the ability to lead their homes. For example, you have Kim, mother of three and unemployed. Kim moves into public housing and because she has no income, her rent is at minimum $50 a month. Kim qualifies and receives food stamps in the amount of $579 a month; Medicaid for herself and the children (free healthcare...priceless). Kim is given childcare vouchers to look for employment and will be granted child care in most states if she is enrolled as a full-time student in an accredited college. You meet Kim and you are in the same situation except you don't have custody of your children and receive no services. You stay with Kim from time to time except when housing comes to do an inspection and she tells you to get lost for the day or say you are family visiting. So again, I ask you... first, how can you become the leader of a home that is not yours? The house is being leased to Kim and is paid by government subsidies (taxpayer's dollars). Second, how can you compete with a system that will give a woman, your woman, all of the basic necessities of life (shelter, food, etc.)? Where is her loyalty? Can you provide for her in this matter? Most men only qualify for such services when they've lost everything to a life of drug and alcohol abuse or declared to have some kind of mental illness or disability. This results in a system that makes poor fathers useless and unneeded impediments to housing and other assistance women receive from the government.

For some of you who are reading this book, you have come to your wits end and you're thinking your situation could not possibly get any worse. If that is you then the only place to go from here is up. It is out of compassion for your struggle that this book has been dedicated to young men between the ages of 17 to 35. Read it and pass it on. Talk to young fathers and men who are at risk of having a child before they are ready about this book. It is critical that each man learns what it takes to be disciplined enough to avoid unwanted pregnancy, caring enough to be a good father and furthermore, teach someone else what he has learned. This book is one step toward helping us transform our families and thus our communities.

Don't You Hate Being Told What to Do?

There is a phrase that goes like this—IF you do what you NEED to do WHEN you NEED to do it, the time will come WHEN you can do what you WANT to do WHEN you WANT to do it. This is a simple yet profound phrase that should become your motto. PROCRASTINATION IS AN ENEMY OF TIME. If you deem yourself responsible, no one should have to tell you when to visit or what to pay for concerning the children that you helped to bring into this world. When it is all said and done, it is you that will be held accountable for what God have given you stewardship over, not the courts.

As men, you hate being told what to do, however if you choose to ignore your responsibility to your children and play dead you will find yourself in a situation where you are made to do what others tell you to do. If you do not want your fatherhood managed by the government, you must demonstrate your intention to be a supportive father financially and otherwise. If you don't, your parental authority will be managed by the government. You must actively support your child before you are taken to court.

If you have not been the best father you can be up to this point, you still have a chance to become the world's greatest dad. We all make mistakes; however, it is what we do to recover from those mistakes that make the difference. If you have not been the best father you can be, it is time for a reality check. You must do better and you can. Make a plan for who you want to become as a father and work toward that goal daily. This will take time, patience, and a do or die commitment that comes from the heart. It is my hope that this book be a light unto your path as you travel along your journey.

CHAPTER ONE
The Relationship

The two of you were cordial at one time; respectful and excited to see one another. You laughed, joked, and engaged in decent dialogue. However, after some time and a baby, the relationship soured. It may not have been your plan to have a child which makes you bitter with your child's mother. Whatever reason you have for not communicating with your child's mother in a productive manner you must get past those feelings. Regardless of your prior plans, a child is here and you two must become partners in order to successfully raise your children.

The relationship between you and your child's mother is the most important factor in determining how well your experience as a parent will be. Even if you are the most loving, supportive father in the world, if you have a poor relationship with your child's mother, she will likely make your experience as difficult as she possibly can. Be proactive. Take the lead. Establish a loving, supportive relationship with your child's mother by being a good communicator and being active in your child's life. Do not underestimate the value of the relationship with your child's mother. This relationship will not only affect your experience as a parent, but it will also affect the quality of your child's upbringing. If for no other reason, establish a good relationship with your child's mother for the sake of your child.

Chapter One: The Relationship

Every ounce of energy you have should be focused on establishing a loving, respectful, and supportive relationship with your parent-partner.

Let's take a look at a few scenarios that may help you understand this relationship component better.

Scenario:

I am in graduate school on the weekends, and I am paying $500 for a babysitter to watch the boys on the weekends. The father is currently paying me $50 a week (for two children) because this is what he could afford at the time. No problem, I thought. I came up with a brilliant plan and brought it to him. I said, since I am paying $500 for childcare every weekend, I can stop paying that if you watch the boys on the weekend and you CAN STOP PAYING YOUR $200 A MONTH. We both win, and the kids get to be with their dad every weekend. I save $300 a month and he saves $200 a month. Brilliant, right; do you want to know what his response was? He said and I quote, "No, that is not going to work for me, because I am going to start dating again and I want to get my life back." After his comment, I said, "Oh okay, so you want to go to child support court." He said, and I quote, "Yes, take me to court because you will not get much more than you're getting now." I said, "Wow! I was trying to help you out at the same time helping the kids and myself as well."

Needless to say, I took him to court and he paid almost $500 additional dollars a month on top of what he was already paying. Were there legitimate reasons he refused my offer? If so, I don't know what they were. I do know we were going through a bad separation and he would make sure that he would not support anything that looked like it would help me get to the next level. He told me that no matter how much school I had, he would always make more money than me. He saw my obtaining my education, running my own business and achieving all that I was accomplishing, as a threat.

This is where you don't want to be my brother. Go to therapy, group sessions or for crying out loud, go to the Cross because those are issues that you will have to work out within yourself. You should not be bothered by your woman's success if you are doing all you can to become successful as well. This situation was avoidable. It was not my intention to extract money from him that he couldn't afford. The fact that he was not willing to come to an agreement dictated my action and his increased dissatisfaction. By reading that, you may see obvious clues which state that he was still very angry and hurt by the separation. However, his anger blurred his ability to make a sound and practical decision. He was not able to keep his eyes on the prize–his children. Let him be the example of how important it is to have a high Emotional Intelligence (EQ). Our EQ is simply the ability to recognize, evaluate, and command mastery of our emotions and those of others. This takes discipline and a very mature heart. My definition of EQ is when the heart and mind flow on the same accord, whereas they both strengthen one another to stay the course; neither one will allow the other to become distracted—thus producing oneness of strength and high actionable intelligence.

Have you ever seen bumper stickers which read "Don't breed them if you can't afford them"? The moment I came across not one but three was when I received the light bulb moment. Ironically enough, welfare was the first place that I was told to go when I found out I was pregnant; not the father's parents but the government. That is when I realized that it was inherently a part of the culture I grew up around. I was ashamed that taxpayer dollars had become the main source of sustenance for me as a result of my poor decision making? That is when I realized that my thinking had to change. We really should not have children that we ourselves cannot afford. I decided that I would do everything in my power to rid myself of the dependency on government assistance and become a self-reliant mother.

*NOTE TO SELF: Avoid unplanned pregnancy

The absolute sure thing to prevent having to go to child support court is to not have any children. The sure way to prevent children is through abstinence or having "the procedure". You know what "the procedure" is? A Vasectomy! And then, of course, there is the pull-out method which is not safe; neither is it a sure way to prevent pregnancy. Then there are condoms that only work ninety-nine (99) percent of the time, if and when you use them. Take control over whether you have children or not! Don't leave it up to the woman to be responsible for birth control. Be responsible! Children cost money and are a life-time responsibility on you and others. If you are not ready to be a parent, be smart- don't create children! Do everything in your power to prevent pregnancy. Abstain from sex or use a condom.

*NOTE TO SELF: Obey God's Law

Your ignorance (lack of knowledge) of a thing does not exempt you from its consequences or effects. For example, let's take the law of gravity. It's a natural law. Whether or not you believe it works does not exempt you from its effects. If you are in a plane and jump out, you are going to fall to the ground unless you have some special device that was created to counteract those effects like a parachute.

Just the same, there are divine principles and laws at work with or without your acknowledgement or permission. Did you know that every time you lay with a woman, in Gods eyes, she is your wife? Now those set of eyes might not mean much to you, but one day they will mean everything. Let me repeat that statement, when you lie down with a woman, she has become one with you. It is not the marriage certificate (the piece of paper) that makes you married; it's when the two of you consummate your marriage through sex.

Sex was only permitted for marriage. I know everyone talks about it and it seems like everyone is doing it but just like you can't drive without a driver's license, technically we should not be having sex without a license–a marriage license. Like many adults, I wish I would have had that revelation growing up. Because when I received that revelation, I already had one child. My ability to abstain was a struggle with evidence of me having three more children. I wish I could go back and wait until I was married to have sex. It wasn't until four kids later I was able to transform my thinking. I ask that you value sex for its intimate and spiritual nature. Honoring the divinity inherent in sex helps us to be more disciplined in terms of how we have sex and who we have sex with. Abstaining from sex until marriage shows your obedience to God, and is the only 100% proven method to prevent unwanted pregnancy with a woman you have no plans to be with for the rest of your life.

If you have low self-worth, you will attract women who are like that as well. That is why searching for the right partner starts with who you are in your heart. Confident men and women who value themselves and have high self-worth do not take serious interests in others who don't. These attributes are in some cases visible while others are not as visible. For example, you see a chick that doesn't take care of herself; you may assume that she is suffering from personal issues. At the same time, you may see a female that dresses nice, and always has her hair done, yet still be plagued with mental and emotional issues. You have to value yourself enough to choose a mate wisely, and for heaven's sake don't be fooled. Everything that glitters isn't gold, and everything that feels good is not good for you. What I am trying to tell you my brother is that today everybody is dealing with something. Women, like men with issues, take their issues from past relationships with them into the new relationships.

Avoid women who you identify as not having the character and qualities you would want in a wife or parent-partner. Understand that you attract what you are. If the woman you deal with is crazy, chances are you are crazy as well.

If you are having issues yourself, seek help before getting into a relationship. The objective is to grow away from the drama caused by dishonest, fickle relationships that lack substance. If you are involved in a relationship that you believe has no future, you are setting yourself up for a trap. Remember, there is no escape from being a parent. Be sure you choose when to become one, and who to become one with, after all, becoming a parent is forever.

This message applies to adults as well as youth; however, this message cannot be more relevant for teenagers. As a teenager, you have so much of your life ahead of you. Waiting to have sex is an investment in your future. Save your body. Having sex puts you at risk for sexually transmitted diseases that you may have for the rest of your life, and potentially pass on to your children. It also puts you at risk of becoming a parent before you are ready. Remember, a few minutes of pleasure can add up to a lifetime of agony. Make the right decision for you–abstain from sex. Many young lives have been ruined due to unplanned pregnancy and sexually transmitted diseases. If you think ahead you will be able to understand why many adults wish they could go back to their youth and save themselves for marriage.

*NOTE TO SELF: Find a mentor

Knowledge is half the battle of life. People perish because of a lack of knowledge, not because knowledge isn't accessible- because it is rejected, refused and not recognized. We are living in the "Information Age" where knowledge has never been more readily available to us; however, there are still so many who have not reached out to grab a hold of it. For those who have reached out for more knowledge, the challenge is applying that knowledge every day.

Applying knowledge is more difficult than obtaining knowledge. No matter your profession, it takes a good teacher to impart knowledge and an even greater one to show you how to apply that knowledge in day-to-day real-life situations. Just as we need mentorship and guidance in our professions, we need mentorship and guidance in everyday life. Find a mentor that is living an exemplary life in terms of fatherhood or in a particular profession. They will elevate the likelihood of you living the life, you planned for yourself by holding you accountable to the information you have learned and applied. Being a good father is not easy. You will need help. I encourage you to find a mentor that can help you be the father and man you want to be.

Love understanding and heed to instruction. Love the fact that there are others who have already fallen into the same traps that await you and are willing to let you know where those traps are. If a person tells you that trouble awaits you up the road and you don't-listen then it is your fault if you continue down the same path. The burden becomes yours and yours alone. Living a healthy life is about making sound choices, and mentorship lends a helping hand in doing just that.

The nature or mechanics of your relationship will determine the plan of action you incorporate. Every strategy will not work with every woman and every situation requires a different strategy. Most men believe that women are too complex to understand. This is not entirely true. Women can be simple if you understand how they are wired. Once you see how they are wired to compliment and help you, the battle is half way won. We will talk in depth on understanding the type of woman you have in chapter two. The emphasis is that you know the basics of what drives women internally in what I like to call "Woman Wiring 101". Whether you had a one-night stand or a committed relationship there are fundamental principles that men should follow to better relate with women.

I have summed up what you need to do to improve your relationship building skills in acronyms called CIA. What is CIA? CIA is a commitment to becoming effective in "communication", "investigation" and "active-listening". But before we get further into our CIA training, let's take a look at the wiring of a woman.

CHAPTER TWO
The Wiring of a Woman

Understand that every woman is wired differently, but the same basic wiring can be found in most sane women. Women are highly emotional beings. To maintain positive, productive relationships with a woman one must be ever conscious of her feelings. Though women are wired for emotion, most women are rational, stable beings and should be approached in a rational, yet tender manner. However, if your child's mother has issues beyond reconciliation or you know her to be crazy and deranged this may not work with her. There may be no way of conveying logic to this type of woman. If she is bleaching your clothes, slashing tires, and breaking windows, your relationship may be too far gone to salvage, but let's not give up hope. If you get this chapter down-pack, you may prevent being sued for child support and other vindictive actions of the scorned woman by keeping her from becoming the scorned woman in the first place.

Emotions are strong feelings that are usually attached to various types of situations, experiences, thoughts, words, etc. I have learned early on that the heart only knows one thing and that is to love. Hate is simply love in reverse or for a better phrase, love that has been hurt. So, the anger she shows towards you is coming from a place of hurt love. Love that has been hurt for a long time grows cold, harbors resentment and feeds unhappiness. The longer you ignore her reasons for being angry at you without addressing what is bothering her, her anger is likely to fester like an infection. You must validate her reasons even if you disagree with them. I'm not telling you to agree with her reasons. Simply confirm that you understand her reasons for feeling that way and ask her what you can do to make her feel better. When you take the path of least resistance you close the door to anger for it can no longer be fed. The chances of you two having productive communication dramatically increases the less the two of you argue.

A woman needs affection. This is not optional. This is basic wiring. Affection means to be acted upon, moved or touched in an emotional capacity. For many women it is the desire for affection that lures her into the arms of someone who does not deserve or abuses her. Once this affection is hurt or betrayed, it is the same affection that will turn cold like stone while she makes your life a living hell. For many women it is this need for affection that leaves them vulnerable to irrational emotions. Your objective is to understand this and act accordingly. Be sensitive and responsive to her needs. Nurture the things that she values so that positive feelings and behaviors are reciprocated.

LET'S ROLEPLAY:

She listens to a voicemail (women are infamous for checking voicemails and finding out your passwords), she hears a message from a lady who says she met you at this place... be it the club, bar, restaurant... doesn't matter at this point. You gave her your phone number. Now, you and your girlfriend have been having mad problems and you are fed up and decided that you just don't give a flying saucer right now. So now, the two of you begin to argue and you can't seem to understand why she is beefing. She is hurt, angry and pissed off that you are talking to other women long enough to give them your phone number knowing full well she would check your voicemail. Why would you do that? You are well aware of what will happen next. You know she checks your voicemail and therefore you intentionally give your number out and send the call to the voicemail. The GAMES PEOPLE PLAY! These are the actions of an immature heart... Man Up!

At this point someone has to raise the level of communication. This is real life, real love and real pain. No one wants to play games. So let's do it again but on the other foot. If she came in with the phone number, you would probably go to the left on her. Then you'll say something like "Okay, you want to play games, I got you" and

Chapter Two: The Wiring of a Woman

then you go out and actually act upon those intentions you have had all along. Now the relationship is breached far past repair. She has a couple of your children... they see the two of you fighting all the time so you decide to leave.

Now it is what happens right here that will decide whether or not you will suffer the scorn of a woman. This is the time you should be talking with other men who are in stable, committed relationships, not your boys who hit the club every weekend starting on Thursday and ending on Sunday. Gain knowledge from an experienced male in the form of advice. Don't be afraid to talk to someone about your situation in order to plan strategically on how you will act going forward. They will tell you to keep your lines of communication open and honest, and do everything in your power to be supportive and not generate her scorn.

NOTE TO SELF:

The worst thing you can do to a woman is to underestimate her intelligence. Don't play her stupid, she wasn't born yesterday. A woman might spazz out initially when she hears the truth (because it hurts), but she can take it and more importantly she will respect you for it. Cowards lie and run from the truth. Remember that!

You don't want to be the coward. She will then lose all respect for you and will make this very clear. When the rubber hits the road, she will respect the fact that you told the truth. Most women, who have had negative experiences with men, expect them to lie and be unfaithful. You might believe that women can't handle the truth. This is a lie and I will need for you to never believe anything like that ever again. Be sure as a man that you are capable and able to handle telling the truth. Because we're often taught to cover up our mistakes with lies, we are trained to run from the truth, but remember it is the truth that sets us free. It forces people to deal with reality opposed to being caught up in the confusion and anger that dishonesty creates. This confusion is caused when a woman's heart wants to believe the lie's that her mind refuses as truth. Remember we are getting free from the bondage one rope at a time, therefore put lies far from your lips and say what you mean, but more importantly mean what you say. Your word is all you have. Brothers understand that the truth should be told in love. Don't wrap truth in garments of sarcasm, criticism and mockery. The true intentions of your heart will be shown when it speaks. Out of the abundance of your heart, your mouth speaks[1]. Don't let your words create contention for a soft answer will turn away wrath[2].

---

1 Luke 6:45 The Holy Bible.
2 Proverbs 15:1 The Holy Bible

Chapter Two: The Wiring of a Woman

Praise her for being smart and let her know that you do appreciate her, but then tell her that you let your flesh get the best of you and you see some areas where you have to mature. Apologize and validate her anger and say, "If I were you, I would be upset too. I would probably never speak to me again." Remember that when an offense is new, it is best to ask for forgiveness right away. Don't, and I repeat don't, let the sun go down on your wrath[3] building inside of your parent-partner or girlfriend. Immediately seek a remedy to the problem and pursue peace at all cost. Although she is very angry, remember a kind word will turn away wrath.

Women are simply wired differently and therefore you will never win an argument debate or discussion with us, so don't even try. If you happen to win one of those debates which may be rarely and she admits that you are right, you have absolutely earned it and have the traits of being a great communicator. Women want you to listen and adhere to the suggestions she recommends because she believes in her heart that she is right. You my brother must lay your pride and ego aside to embrace the gift that God has given you. Learn

---

3 Ephesians 4:26 The Holy Bible.

of her ways; learn how she operates so you can best utilize all she has to offer. Smart men understand this and are victorious in every area of their lives because they have worked this simple yet profound principle. You have to admit that God made women pretty smart and intuitive. Yes, she is often blinded by her emotions and may react in a totally irrational manner; however, your job is to strengthen who you are emotionally by increasing your EQ. Most of us were not taught this therefore we cannot expect it to come second nature and or happen overnight. Being strong and patient will prove favorable for you in the end.

When you come clean from the heart, there is nothing she can push against. Women were created with a special ability to multi-task. She can be doing five, six or seven things, guaranteed she is still paying close attention to you. Women never really forget things. Because they are very emotional, they usually always tie situations, circumstances, words, and or experiences into a mental note and or a feeling that they won't ever forget. Instead of arguing over the details of what was said in previous conversations, move forward and address what changes regarding your relationship need to be established. Say something more like, "Did I say that? Wow! I really don't remember. If I said it, that was not what I intended to say.

Chapter Two: The Wiring of a Woman

What I meant to say was ..." This will give you the opportunity to de-escalate the argument and restate your message in a manner that won't be twisted or confused. This allows the both of you to move forward and create a new reality.

Understand this book is not to be critical of your decisions, but rather to help you create a drama free life and prevent you from stepping on the land mines that are set before you. There are no quickies in the arenas of relationship building and effective communication. Improving in these areas will require you to use tact and most importantly require that you are authentic and sincere. There are men who believe that it is easier to keep running and ignore the fact that they are a father to a child or multiple children. Men who choose to ignore their paternal responsibility choose a life of child support litigation, drama, bondage and possible imprisonment.

Now running looks different for every man. Some men vanish and do what I call the disappearing act where the child or parent never sees you again... If this is you then shame on you! There are some men who are considered to be seasonal or part time (as needed when needed). These men call on birthdays and major holidays and visit once or twice a year or even monthly. Then there are those who make every attempt to be an active father but are pushed away by domineering and controlling angry women who aim to make their lives a living hell.

Some men believe that because a woman was quick to lay down with them she has done this before with several other men. This is probably true in some cases, but not all. And, if you believe that she has been around the block too many times, why on earth would you have sex with her without protection? Have you ever heard of delaying instant gratification? Denying yourself makes you stronger mentally, emotionally and physically. You will have to D.I.G. deep within yourself to find the courage and wisdom to do it. Once you are strong mentally, everything else eventually will line up. Besides if you play the tape all the way to the end and count your costs you will see that the decision to have sex without protection may be a lifetime of unnecessary agony. I'm confident you will come up with enough reasons to at least put on a condom. If you believe a woman is not worthy to be the mother of your child, don't have unprotected sex with her. As simple as this may sound, a woman not worthy to be the mother of your child is not worthy to have sex with.

Remember the movie Friday when Smokey said, "Don't you ever, ever, ever, ever, ever come round here"? Well, I will tell you that when you find out that the woman you had sex with announces she is pregnant, don't you ever, ever, ever, ever, ever say, "That baby is not mine!" or ask "Who is the daddy?" in your the ignorant voice. Regardless of how you feel about the possibility of the child not being yours, you had better know she is going to be upset and feel disrespected by your questioning. Seriously, this is the worst thing she could hear at this moment. Instantly she will position her heart against you. Chances are if she says the baby is yours, it is, and you will have hurt her immeasurably. A hurt woman will either lash out immediately or harm you further down the line through some act of vengeance if you do not do your due diligence in repairing that breach in your relationship.

WHAT YOU WANT TO SAY:

If you are faced with the situation of possible fatherhood say the following, "Listen love, you and I know we had no intentions of having a child, but because neither one of us did anything to prevent it, I will do all that I can to support you in your decision." I'm willing to bet a month's paycheck that you will gain so much respect from her that you would have to act like a complete fool to mess that relationship up. Instantly you have positioned her heart towards you. Women will deduct points for actions that show a lack of support or irresponsibility, but absolutely grant points for every small act of support that you show and you will never know it. These are her mental notes. Before you respond to a situation trust that she has already practiced and played the scenario in detail in her head and has considered all possible reactions. She will not expect you to be supportive unless you are already a supportive type of dude; otherwise she is expecting you to be angry and say something that will hurt her. She really wants you to be cool, if not happy and honored, with the idea of her having your baby. Be positive and supportive from the beginning and you will be well on the way to establishing a great relationship with her parent-partner.

Women are uniquely different, each having something very special about them. When men validate this difference and confirm their uniqueness then the sky's the limit. For every woman you encounter, the first thing you should think about is, "What is different about this woman and what difference will she make in my life?" Along with paying more attention to the needs of the mother of your child, let me suggest that you pay more attention to the women you choose to date overall. If you don't realize anything of quality in the woman's character, reconsider establishing any relationship with her. Relationships built on fickle desires often produce unwanted pregnancies by women whom you have a lack of respect for. If you don't respect the women who decided to give birth to your children, then chances of you respecting the purpose in which your children were created to fulfill is slim to none. In your search for a mate, search for a woman who displays qualities you respect and admire.

It is absolutely critical to understand that when the woman is happy—everyone is happy! Talk to any man, not any male, any man who has a successful marriage and family. They will confirm this to be true. Keeping your parent-partner happy is keeping you and your family happy. You don't have to be romantically involved with the mother of your child to have a positive, respectful parent- partner relationship. Yes, it is clear that women can be controlling, extremely manipulative and cunning to say the least. In most cases, she is paying the cost to be the boss; I suggest you do the same.

If you are not observing and gaining insight on who she is and the gifts she has to compliment you, the chances of you missing something is great. Women know when you are paying attention and they also know when and where they can pull a fast one on you.

Now, there are some men who are on top of their "A-game" who are able to stop a woman right in her tracks to let her know that he is aware of everything she is up to. Women love this and find it hilarious and honorable. Woman test men for respect when she senses it is not there. The ability to respect you is seen, felt and clearly understood at the very beginning. She is looking for someone she believes will protect her and make her a priority.

I need for you to get this visual. Women today are like superwoman. She rises early and commences to taking care of the family fort as best as she can with what she has. She fills every gap and often times comes home to someone that has no real idea of the giants she had to slay that day. She wants nothing more than to be able to come home and take her cape off and lay in the arms of her superman. A woman will go to back for the right man who may not always do the right things. Perfection is not what the women desires of you; being a man of your word in deed and action, commanding love, loyalty and respect is what she needs. Your ability to remove her cape and cover her with yours is what the woman desires. Please understand that the world is safer, more stable and productive when superwoman has her superman. Save her, restore her value and most importantly, love her.

CHAPTER THREE
The Art of Communication

This is probably one of my favorite topics, because it is at the core of who we are as human beings. Communication is more than talking and being heard, it is everything from tone of voice and projection, intention, body language, articulation, facial expressions and emphasis on words; all of which are flushed through the heart. A person can interpret a word or phrase in several different ways causing the message to be misunderstood. Most times what is communicated is far different from what is heard. Be sure that you communicate thoughtfully. Avoid being insulting, condescending, rude, or inflammatory. Communication that generates negative emotions prohibits growth and feeds negativity. Using words like "Never" and "Always" are considered roadblocks to communication. The likelihood of someone never or always doing something 100% of the time is a fabrication—one should stay away from these words when communicating.

Every time someone offends you, it is like a pebble or a little stone that enters the heart. Even though we are not aware of these offenses that transpire almost daily, each pebble when joined by others weigh heavily on the heart. This is where you don't want your parent-partner's heart to be—a heavy stone weight. Remember, when our hearts are heavy we carry that burden around everywhere we go. We communicate from a place of hurt, and thus spread our emotions to others making it impossible to have positive, constructive interaction. Hurt people hurt people!

Our ability to communicate from a place that is safe and nurturing allows us to communicate effectively with others even when we are upset and or hurt. When a person realizes that you care about them and communicate with them as such, they are more willing to let down their guards and deal with you in the same manner you deal with them. What we say and do is ever important in determining how we work and communicate with others. Positive communication is our aim. It is communication that transmits positive feelings and works towards a mutually shared goal. Two cannot establish common goals without effective communication. It is important that you are aware of your mental, emotional and spiritual state when communicating; this is critical in resolving disputes and arresting conflicts. Dealing with issues that are highly sensitive, emotional or combative when you are not strong enough is like walking on a land mine.

Communication, Investigation, and Active Listening (CIA)

Let's talk about enhancing your CIA skills and using these three tools to bridge the gaps in your communication.

1. **Communication–**The art of expressing one's thoughts and feelings; to exchange ideas and information in a clear and functional way. Communication can be effective or ineffective. It can mean saying the right things at the right times in the right way; or saying the wrong things at the wrong times in the wrong way. I believe you can catch more bees with honey than you can with vinegar. Let's try communicating the right way today!

2. **Investigation–**To examine or study in detail; to search out the facts about something that appears to be hidden. The number one rule to this skill is learning to ask the right questions. I have learned that many people are afraid of rocking the boat and therefore don't ask the critical questions that if answered correctly will bring peace and assurance to your assumptions. There is no need in thinking something that may be far from the truth if you are not willing to ask.

James 4:2 tells us that we have not because we ask not. We desire various things but refuse to ask for what we want. Understand that it is not so much what you ask but more so how you ask. Your motives should be one that is seeking simply to understand and gain more knowledge. Your refusal and or inability to ask questions show a disinterest in the situation or fear in the circumstance at hand.

Investigation is similar to critical thinking. The ability to clarify your goals, evaluate your evidence or findings and ask the right questions are critical to you obtaining all the information you will need to make an intelligent decision. Making assumptions and drawing conclusions without doing a thorough investigation is foolish. If you are not willing to take the time and put in the work; you will consistently rely on others to supply you with vital information you need to change your life.

3. **Active Listening-**The art of not simply hearing words but listening with an attentive ear to hear what types of words she is using, the tone in which she is using them, and the emphasis on certain words over the other. Reading body

language and facial expressions are also critical components of active listening. Active listening does not attempt to be understood. Active listening involves seeking to understand. It is paraphrasing what you thought you heard and giving constant feedback which ensures her that you are being attentive.

Active listening is neutral. It does not offend nor does it defend. When you listen actively you are listening to what is being said, the emotion behind what is being said, and what is gathered when reading between the lines; all without trying to respond or thinking about what you will say when given the chance. When you actively–listen you will do nothing but listen and ask questions when and where appropriate to gain further insight. Understanding how people are feeling and the thoughts they are trying to convey will help you satisfy or at least accommodate their needs.

If your significant other has ever said, "You don't listen," she is not saying you don't hear her speaking; she knows you are not deaf or she would be communicating to you in sign language. What she is saying goes far beyond words. She just wishes you would listen more attentively and begin to plug the pieces of her communication puzzle together.

Women communicate in such a way whereas it is continual like a sequel. If you are just deciding to tune into her channel, there is no doubt you will be lost. You will have to watch previous episodes from past seasons to understand what is going on in this current scene of her life. When you don't stay on the scene long enough and you decide to flip channels, you will miss the best part.

If she has been with you for some time, she expects for you to have observed her behaviors and begin putting one and two together. The object to actively listening is staying connected to her plot. I told you this would be challenging; however these skills make all the difference in managing good relationships and strengthening cooperation.

Be aware that hurt feelings fuel poor communication and if left to fester will totally disintegrate your relationship. Listen for hurt feelings. Communicate out of love to remove hurt feelings. If she is angry with you, for whatever reason, you already know that you have a lot of work ahead of you to win back her trust. Start now. The benefits of winning back her trust and re-establishing your relationship as a parent partnership will benefit you in the end.

Positive communication, particularly in negatively charged emotional situations, requires you to really step up your EQ game. We learned that EQ calls for an individual to think, speak, and act rationally. Emotions are the cause of poor decision-making which leads to poor communication and poor life outcomes. I beg you to think and be committed to increasing your EQ.

Do you let your negative feelings, or the negative feelings of others control you in a manner that leads you to make poor decisions? If so, it is time for a change. From now on, I hope you will think for yourself and refuse to be misled by your emotions. You can no longer allow your parent-partner or anybody else for that matter to control your actions through their negativity. Think ahead to the consequences of your decisions and always work toward the best possible outcome for your circumstance. Becoming stronger emotionally means you become stronger mentally.

Do you have to be a scholar to do this? The answer is no. You just have to be in touch with where you are in your relationship and where you want to be. The best communicator is one who is not easily angered; one who does not blurt out everything that is on his heart and one who uses discretion in his choice of words. A great communicator is quick to hear and slow to speak.

Keep in mind that you should communicate with purpose—relaying information and receiving information as it was intended to be communicated. Be positive even in the midst of negative feelings to ensure that the way you communicate keeps you on the path of satisfying your needs as well as the needs of your parent-partner. Communicate in a way that builds the relationship, not in a manner that tears it down.

There is some reciprocity necessary to make these things work. If communicating and working together was a one-way street we probably would not be having this conversation. According to Webster's Dictionary, the word "reciprocity" is defined as "to match or complement; to give and return mutually." Relationships require this ingredient. As you give, you should expect for her to give as well. For as long as the earth remains; there will be seed time and harvest—a sowing and reaping. If you sow positive seeds—positivity you should receive. A seed can only produce after its own kind. An apple seed will never produce an orange, just as a seed of love, joy and peace will only produce that which it is.

If your parent-partner is not being a good partner in terms of working and communicating with you, she may need just as much support as you do. Being a good parent-partner requires commitment and work. It is not something that will happen overnight, but communicate with her that you would like to establish with her a healthy partnership in raising your child. If she is not receptive to your honesty, communication, and support, you may have no other option but to take legal action. Let's face it; every woman is not a good person or parent. Legal action is not only to be exercised by women. Men, do not be afraid to take your child's mother to court in order to have your parental rights honored. In fact, this is recommended if your parent-partner refuses to let you see your children for her own illegitimate reasons.

Some men are in a place right now where they have a restraining order against them by their child's mother which prevents open communication with the mother and child. In this case, you must still do everything in your power to be a good man and father. First, seek change from within to get away from what led her to request a restraining order against you. Did you lose your temper, or was she retaliating? Either way the victory takes place from the inside out. Meanwhile, seek legal representation. There are agencies that provide free legal services that will fight for your cause as the father who wants to be more involved in your child's life. We've all made mistakes. Perfection is not a requirement to be a parent, but being present and supportive is. Seek representation that will fight for your ability to get past the restraining order so that you can be more present and supportive in your child's life.

Seek a win-win situation that satisfies you and your child's mother in terms of providing for the child. No matter what your differences are, you can at least agree that you don't want to be dragged through the child support system. Its intrusiveness and wage garnishments cause just as much damage to you as being a single mother raising a child alone does to her. You both must be willing to sacrifice for the child's well-being. The only thing left to do is communicate and come to agreement about financial arrangements, day care, custody and all matters concerning the child. At some point, someone will have to lay down their swords, cease the cutting and begin to mend and heal the wounds. If for no other reason than to teach the children how to work through difficult situations.

To communicate successfully you must first be empathetic. Try and understand what your parent-partner wants, what hurts her, and what makes her happy. Satisfy her desires as much as possible, and avoid making her upset. Most women are primarily concerned with the welfare of their children above petty drama, so be as supportive as possible as early as possible in your child's life. Your relationship with your parent-partner is the single most important factor in deciding the degree to which you become involved in the child support system. Even if you don't have a good relationship with your child's mother, there is no excuse for you to be absent. If you are absent, it is just a matter of time before the child support system takes control of your parenthood. Communicating and being active in your child's life will make putting you on child support unnecessary and unlikely. When the woman sees that you are doing all that you can do for the well-being of your children, she will not drag you through the courts. If you are going through the court system and being sued for child support, I will simply ask you to consider your ways.

I believe if you are reading this book, God has a plan for your life and it is does not include you doing what you've done in the past. Are you committed to the work—the inward transformation that has the power to change your entire reality for the better? Many of you are ready for this transformation. You have tried everything else and it all failed. You have spent a lot of money, but you haven't much to show for it. You keep filling your plates, but you never get filled up. You keep drinking and drinking and drinking, but you're always thirsty. You put on layer after layer of clothes, but you can't get warm, you earn wages to put them in a bag with holes in it. Take a good, hard look at your life and think it over[4]. You must change the way you think about fatherhood. Be a supportive father and parent-partner because it is the right thing to do, and you will be well on your way to avoiding the traps of the child support system.

I know you are thinking, "I thought she was going to tell me how to stay out of child support court. This sounds a lot different." In fact, communicating and building relationships are critical to staying out of child support court. The inability to communicate and build positive relationships is what leads to the adversarial relationship with your child's mother that is sure to land you in child support. This understanding is central to getting the child support court out of your pockets.

Now there are many men who are doing the right thing but it seems as though the system will not let up and more importantly the mother of your child is not trying to hear anything else but, "Show me the money!" If you continue to do the right thing, not just so you can get what you want, but because it's simply the right thing; your situation will change, especially if you are deliberate and strategic on

---

4 Haggai 1:6-7 The Holy Bible.

how you provide support, communicate with your parent-partner, and spend time with your child. Ultimately, however, you may need legal representation.

Reading this, you may be thinking "this is too much work"! "I'm not doing all of that". Then I would ask, if what you've been doing—working out for you? Doing the same thing and expecting different results is INSANITY! If what you are doing is working for you, then there is no need to change. However, if your life has any evidence of failed intentions and broken promises then you might want to consider a different route.

CHAPTER FOUR
The Dilemma

I thought the best way to illustrate this chapter was to give you a visual of what is really happening when you make haphazard decisions. The first section spells everything out and the next illustrates what is being said. As you follow the diagram, look at your own life and see where you have made the same or similar decisions and see how things could possibly end. The outcomes may not result in a positive, happy ending if there is no change in your behavior. It is not easy to make the right decision when the right decision is the tougher road that requires more sacrifice. However, I ask that you are aware of the dilemmas that you may face, and to always make the right decision for the sake of your children. Just as there are many different relationship dynamics, there are many different dilemmas.

Here is the most classic example of a dilemma:

1. Okay, you meet a young lady, at the park, restaurant, movies, club, or church—right? For whatever reason, you both rush into sex. Wow, now it's over, that was quick! A month or so later, you discover that she's pregnant. You could have said "no" to sex or you could have used protection but you chose not to do either. You chose to sow your seed within the womb of a woman you barely knew. You made a decision that will change your life forever.

Chapter Four: The Dilemma

She's off to obtain support from various government programs all of which are supported through taxpayer's dollars. What you don't know is that the welfare system has made a provision in their policies for absent dads who have not provided parental support. They will always ask the woman your whereabouts. If she has a good relationship with you, one built on trust and respect, she will either tell them the truth or lie. She will let them know that yes, you provide support for the children she is seeking assistance for or no you don't provide any assistance at all. Lying on the application is considered a federal offense, so best believe your full government name; address and social security number is going on the application, even if she has doubts on who the father of her child is. Depending on what she says will determine if you get a visit from the sheriff's office. She may already be planning to take you to child support. For most women, this is a last resort.

So you act like the baby is not yours, walk off, give her the peace sign. She is angry, hurt and rejected and she is already planning on seeing you in child support court or locked up.

The baby arrives and she is trying to give you a second chance, she calls you but you don't return her call. She phones your momma's house to tell them the baby was born and they don't seem to care. She sends you several texts that go unanswered. She wants to show you this beautiful bundle of love that the both of you participated in creating. As she looks into the eyes of the most precious gift (your child), she is filled with hope for the child's future, love for the child itself and a desire to have her child NOT grow up without a father. What do you do? Would you do absolutely nothing, or make the effort and go and see your child?

You see her and the baby and the first thing you think to yourself, this baby is not even mine. You decide to play it cool because you are totally at a loss as to what this really means. She may have thoughts and hopes of the two of you getting back together to raise a family. Although this may be the farthest thing from your mind; understanding that children change the dynamics of relationships and you will have to stand up and be a father or be faced with the consequences.

Chapter Four: The Dilemma

2. Child support papers are filed and you have officially been served. Trifling men will avoid showing up for court and dodge the constable, but a real man will confront the system and his responsibility. You answer the petition and show up to the court.

   - *How are you dressed?*
   - *Do you have a job?*
   - *Are you in school?*
   - *Do you have documentation of your income?*
   - *Do you have a written plan of action to show how you will support the child/children, if in fact you are proven to be the father of the child?*
   - *Are you disabled and cannot work and therefore you bring documentation to show this?*

If you answer NO to the questions above, then the chances of you showing up to the court properly prepared to represent yourself are slim to none.

The Judge does not even let you say two words, or explain your situation. In fact, he/she shuts you down after your first three words, "umm, your honor". You know why? Because there is nothing you can say! A good judge will point you in the direction of programs and services that will help you become a better father. A regular judge will simply order the judgment against you and/or send you to jail. You leave the court pissed off. For what, who are you really angry with?

The objective here is to inspire you to be proactive and take care of your responsibilities before being summoned to court. If you are responsible from the beginning (keeping receipts and a journal which logs your activities with your children) and get summoned to child support court at a later date, the judge is much more likely to be more lenient with you and hear your side.

3. At this point, she has changed hundreds of diapers, missed quality time in school or with friends. She has had little sleep and can find no time to do anything but take care of the baby. This is not the time you will find mercy. Mercy doesn't live there. At this point, you will need to call that someone who can add some super to your natural. Because by this time...

She is smiling–saying show me the money. She doesn't even care and she sure as heck doesn't want to consider you coming back into her life because you got a revelation that it is cheaper to keep her. She has your money on her mind, because you gave her no other choice. She even has the baby saying "cha-ching". I know you are saying, "But I don't have any money." It's not about the money honey. She knows you don't have the money. She is getting pleasure out of making your life a living hell. Why? Because, you have been the primary source of her frustration and struggle.

Now you are stuck, like a fat man in a telephone booth. You are either angry and you won't pay, broke and can't pay, or will work off the books to avoid paying. Even if you are working a nine to five, after child support, you're really broke. There is no place for you to go when child support jacks half your paycheck. Don't be the player—player type of man and find yourself in the same situation with another woman; DUDE you're going to be broke forever and you are causing a curse upon your life, it's called "inheriting the wind". Every time you get something, it will only be a matter of time before it blows right from your hands. You think this is life; no this is life under a curse. A man that brings trouble to his family will inherit the winds (Proverbs 11:29).

Just because you fail to acknowledge your family (your children) does not negate your responsibility to them nor does it excuse the curse from your life.

4. So you are not the responsible father, and therefore you don't show up in court. A warrant is issued for your arrest. You get locked up for failure to pay child support. This is not a good look and the judge is less likely to show you mercy once you show up in his or her courtroom. Once you get out, you begin feeling the pressure of finding employment with an arrest that will show up when a criminal background is conducted. What are the odds of you getting this job? This is how the employer looks at it: If you won't tend to or take care of the needs of a human being who is helpless and in need of your support, how will you take care of the needs of that business?

You are fired before you are hired!

In case you did not get the memo, we are in a global market. What does that mean? That means that the trading between countries is easy, an employer can do business with China just as easy as it can with a local business. The barriers to trade are lifted, and manufacturing jobs are leaving the country at an alarming rate. What does this have to do with you? Listen carefully! Employers are able to conduct business with individuals in India and pay a wage close to three to five dollars an hour, without paying the insurances and taxes that are required in America. The effects of wage garnishments and the impact of nonpayment of child support reduce your opportunities to become employed earning a livable wage.

Here is where you have the power to change your dilemma

5. If you're smart and you are determined to become victorious in life, you must commit yourself to advancing your education to increase your power to earn more money. When I say focus on advancing your education that may mean different things to different people. That could mean vocational training, on-the-job-training, GED program, community college, or four-year college degree. Choose a route that is connected to your passion and purpose. You have read the statistics of those who were struggling with child support payments; more than half of them dropped out of high school.

Whatever the case may be, choose where you want to go in life and follow the game plan that helps you get there. If this place you desire is better than the place you're in now, you can rest assured that it will require more education and knowledge than you have now. Please, know that. Be prepared. You should attack earning more education like never before. There is no question about it. The more education you have the more you will make throughout the course of your life.

Whatever you do, you should not adopt an "I don't care" mentality. Remove the word "NOT" from your life. Phrases like "I am NOT smart enough"; "school is NOT for me"; "I can NOT"; and "I do NOT have the time" keep you in the negative. Make a decision delete the word "NOT" from your vocabulary and watch how you will begin to do things you never thought you could do.

There is a light at the end of the tunnel. Your tunnel may be longer or shorter than others. But thank God for the light. As long as you can see the light, keep walking towards it and eventually you will get there. Advancing your education will increase how much you earn, and that's half the battle in improving your life and being a more supportive father.

The wise man increases knowledge and gains understanding. Going back to school is about acquiring the knowledge and skills that qualify you for higher pay. How else will you become qualified for higher pay without advancing your education? In reference to child support proceedings, enrolling in school or vocational training shows good faith to the judge that you are making an attempt to work and support your child.

Government is an advocate for education and all who choose to lay education aside do so at the expense of their futures. It is almost criminal not to take advantage of the multiple opportunities available to citizens to advance their education. Knowledge is power and the opposite means, "No Knowledge, No Power." When you are powerless to increase your income, you become powerless to decide the quality of life that you and your children will experience.

6. For many of us, it seems as though education is taboo, not necessary or unattainable. People shun education because they think it is un-cool, they don't want to put in the work, or they lack the confidence to try. I urge you to make a major shift in your attitude if this is you. Don't box yourself into economic hardship for the rest of your life. Get out now while you still have a chance and begin working on the plan that will give you the life of your dreams.

School is a safe place. It is a place of knowledge, wealth, and opportunity. It will help you to develop networks with professors, colleagues and business professionals. With the right guidance from advisors and mentors, you will be on track to increase your income. You will be better equipped and qualified to exchange your skills, experience, talents, gifts and wisdom for currency and other sources of wealth.

7. Let's talk about the life of those who believe education is not a fundamental activity in life and therefore choose the life of a hustler. (NOTE: A hustler is someone who lives day by day engaging in either legal or illegal activities to make ends meet). He or she has no long-term sustainable plan for the future. You will know when your plan is sustainable when you remove yourself from it and it continues to grow without you. Your children cannot inherit a hustle. Hustles are short term. Getting a good education, building a solid career, and building wealth over time is where you want to set your sail towards.

After your hustle has landed you in jail or the prison system, it's as if you've tied an anchor around your neck and added miles to your journey. Not understanding who you are and where you fit will cause you to make decisions that are not conducive to your well-being.

Chapter Four: The Dilemma

The prosperity and peace of mind that comes with earning your money legitimately and what that means for your family is priceless. When you take penitentiary chances to make a living, one day that gamble is going to cost you every sacrifice that you have made including your

Let's imagine that you're home, in between jail stays, you may find yourself making the same mistake all over again–having sex with no protection because you've just got to have it. Okay, so now you have about three, four, five kids, with possibly five different women in which you have no real relationship. You find yourself CAUGHT UP!

The vicious cycle begins and the chances of you supporting all of your children are slim. Those who invest in the prison industry are made rich off of the backs of people who think and act like you do. Surely, those who study the clientele of prisons and jails don't believe that you will ever stop making such poor decisions and even if you did, there are thousands of others who will fill your shoes. Have you ever looked at the penal system, judicial (court) system, and criminal justice system? Observe everyone there from the sheriffs, police, lawyers, judges, counselors, aides, etc. Just think to yourself that you are paying their salaries. Without your supply of foolishness, disobedience, irresponsibility, stubbornness, and laziness there would not be such a high demand for police officers, sheriffs, lawyers, judges, probation officers, etc. Listen, as a young man it is absolutely ridiculous for you to spend your time and hard-earned money in the court system. Wise up!

The beautiful part of education is it is accessible for every man, regardless of race, color, and ethnicity. No one can tell you that you cannot learn, and that you cannot read and or acquire knowledge- that choice is yours. Choose the life you want to live. Be smart. Be disciplined. Poor choices cost a lifetime of pain. A good education will pay off for a lifetime.

I remember reading the biography of Harriet Tubman. It stated that back in the day, literacy was a forbidden fruit because if slaves learned how to read and write, they would be able to forge their master's names on their slave documentation and thus free themselves. Slaves were required to carry papers which would verify whether they were legally free or bound. Back then, a black man or woman could lose their life if they were caught reading. Education is and has always been the best opportunity for people to become powerful, increase their earning potential, and enhance their quality of life. Through education, opportunity abounds and an endless stream of green lights awaits you.

Chapter Four: The Dilemma

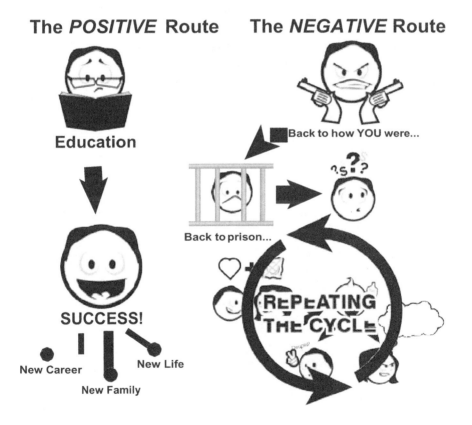

CHAPTER FIVE
The Catch 22

What is the Catch 22? It is a situation where you find yourself between a rock and a hard place. When you are in a Catch 22, it is important that you make no rash or hasty decisions. In the context of child support; the Catch 22 is the place where you find yourself having to choose between unfair treatments with evidence of high child support payments that make it difficult for you to survive as well as dodging the child support system thus providing minimum support for your child and putting yourself at risk of serving jail time.

The system can be unfair; however, I encourage you to stick in there and do the right thing. Set three goals for yourself:

1. Be as supportive to your child/children as possible.
2. Be sure to have legal representation to protect your interests if you do have to appear in court for child support.
Don't allow a bad relationship with your child's mother or your
3. financial troubles to influence you to make poor decisions regarding your children. Be prepared to face tough decisions, and situations that make it difficult for you to support your children the way that you would like to. Most of all, you should be prepared to sacrifice for your children no matter the cost.
4. Create an action plan for your life.

You have heard me mention earlier, the term D.I.G.–Delay Instant Gratification. You must postpone, delay, and prolong the hype of the moment in order to bring your situation into its proper perspective. Instant gratification is the sure road to long-lasting disaster. What seems "right" at the moment often proves to make us cry later. In many cases cry for years. Whether it's unprotected sex or the abuse of drugs, the cost of a mistake due to your lack of discipline could mean a horrifying reality in the future. Unprotected sex can lead to incurable sexually transmitted diseases and unwanted pregnancy. Please, brothers treat your body as a temple. Learning to say "no" will take you a long way toward postponing children until you are married and ready to be the head of your family. When physical desires are gratified immediately, it is often done with no planning or regard for future consequences.

If you delay the satisfaction for five minutes at a time, you would have delayed it for an hour. Delaying it for an hour turns into two. Eventually the time delayed will add up to twelve and twenty-four hours. This is extremely difficult if your mind is constantly thinking about the pleasures the instant gratification will bring you. Changing your thoughts while you practice the D.I.G. technique will be critical to you being successful.

Most often, the only thing that stands between a really dumb decision and a really good decision is TIME! Whatever the situation, play the tape all the way to the end. In other words fast forward and see if you can determine what will happen as a result of your decisions. If the end is not positive then press "Stop"! Pressing the stop button means removing yourself from the scenario. When you decide to press play again you should be somewhere far away from the situation you were in.

The object is to make a habit out of not giving into temptation so easily. D.I.G. will not happen overnight. It is a technique that when practiced, will get better overtime.

For example: At this very moment it is a beautiful Saturday afternoon and I am in the house writing the revisions of this book. My children are with their grandparents and I have the house to myself. I could be doing other enjoyable things. Most young and beautiful women may have chosen to go out on a date, go out with the girls, to the movies, out of town, to the club, or be hugged up with that special someone. While all of these things sound very fun and fulfilling; I am delaying that sense of immediate satisfaction and much pleasure, to do the needful thing.

Chapter Five: The Catch 22

Does this mean that I never do any of the things above? Absolutely not! When I feel the urge to do something, I ask myself will this help me or hurt me, will it bring me closer to my desired place or further away. Anything that takes me further away from my plan in life is something that I typically stay away from.

So you can better understand what a Catch 22 is, I have given you a few scenarios. Read through them and choose the answer that best describes how you would react.

Scenario #1:

You have five children, and you are supporting every one of them. You make a pretty decent salary as a truck driver but after child support deductions you can hardly pay your rent. One of your children's mothers recently requested a "Cost of Living Adjustment" also known as COLA; and now you are required to pay more money than you already pay. In fact, the increase is so much that you won't be able to pay your rent. So, you get a second job to help make ends meet to only find out that Child Support wants to take that income into account as well.

What Do You Do?

A. Quit both jobs, or ask your employers to switch you to an "off the books" status.

B. Request for a modification and file joint custody for all of your children? (Note: Joint custody decreases your child support liability causing you to pay less since you are assuming half of the responsibility). Doing this means that you are willing and able to take on the responsibility of being an active father in the life of your child. You assume responsibility for everything that goes on in your child's life as well as making sure the communication between you and the child's mother is open and modeling the way for positive parenting.

Get a third job.

C. Grumble, curse, and complain because you are so pissed off and

D. you feel powerless against the situation. (In other words, you do nothing and be broke).

E. Move out of state where no one can locate your whereabouts.

If you are forced to choose among of the answer choices above, you are by default in the midst of a Catch 22. The best answer is "B" as the others required you escaping your responsibility. However, I'm

Chapter Five: The Catch 22

not an advocate for anyone filing for joint custody simply because they want to reduce the amount of money they would pay. Although it is a smart move, it requires a great deal of responsibility. Whatever you do, don't try to hide how much you make by getting paid off the books, don't quit working, don't move out of state to evade your responsibilities, and don't accept being treated unfairly by anyone. Answer choice "B" provides the opportunity to reduce your monthly child support payments and become more active in your child's life. This option also helps relieve your parent-partner of some childcare duties. I'm sure she's eager to share.

Scenario #2:
You and your long-time female companion are having trouble. You love her and want to marry her someday. In the midst of your trouble you meet someone that you are very attracted to. You let her know that you recently came out of a relationship but leave out the details that you guys are still trying to work it out. One thing leads to another and the two of you become intimate. The relationship that the two of you have is merely physical. No one is complaining and all seems to be going well until about two months later; she tells you that she is pregnant.

What Do You Do?

A. Tell her the baby is not yours and disappear.

B. Let her know you are not ready to be a father, and ask her to get an abortion and volunteer to pay for it.

C. Ask her what she wants to do and support whatever decision she makes, knowing this could be the end of your previous relationship with the woman you love.

D. Tell her you need some time to get your thoughts together, meantime you rush over to your significant other's house to see how tight the two of you really are in hopes that when you tell her, the two of you together can come up with a game plan (knowing there's a good chance that she will take you back).

E. You do nothing major, just keep things as they have been and figure that you will deal with the baby when it arrives. You continue the same routine you've had and make no new changes.

Any one of these answers has you headed toward child support court except for "C". Your objective here is to communicate and be supportive. Though she may have thoughts of an abortion, the ultimate decision belongs to her. She would only choose the abortion route if she believes that it will make the situation between the two of you better. If she were admittedly opposed to having children, she would have taken the necessary steps to avoid it. For the record, abortion is not a form of contraceptive and it should not be considered a viable alternative to preventing unwanted pregnancies. Therefore, be open and honest in your communication about the matter but at the same time support whatever she decides. Be open and honest to your companion as well. If she is a mature woman, she will still care for you and your child. If she has her head on right and is focused on her business, she would leave you. Your decision to lay down with a woman you barely know and not have enough discipline or sense to use protection is a clear snapshot of your decision-making abilities. However, if she truly loves you–she will try her best to work it out with you; however don't expect it to be easy.

Scenario #3:
The mother of one of your children is having some financial problems. You support your child with no court involvement. She asks if she and your child can stay with you for a couple of months till she gets it together and you say of course, "Yes!" You are making a pretty decent living, you are dating again, and the two of you have decided that what you had is over and you both will do whatever is best for the

child. Six months later, she finally moves out the house and much to your shock, there are some child support documents at your front step. You find out that the child support request dates back to a full year ago, and she never mentioned that she was in the process of suing you for child support.

What Will Likely Happen?

A. After possibly having flashbacks of slapping her, you come to terms with a better way of handling it. You go to court unprepared (no receipts or journals of what you have spent over the course of the six months and no formal agreement in writing explaining the terms and conditions of your arrangement) believing that the Judge will believe your story of her staying with you for six months.

B. Go to court prepared with all the necessary documentation, only to be told by the judge that you still owe the arrears of child support. You are now basically pissed off for life and therefore begin to harbor feelings of resentment towards the mother of your children and this strife between you and the mother keep you and your child apart.

Neither one of the answers are conducive to your peace of mind. The truth of the matter is that most men show up in court unprepared and wonder why they receive an unfavorable decision. While there are times when others show up totally prepared (representing themselves with no attorney) and still receive what seems like an unfair and unjust judgment against them. Always be on your "P's" and "Q's" gentleman. You must begin to act like a man, but think like a woman. A woman plays out every scenario to the end, in her head. Never try to fight a woman in the system without legal representation, and don't let anything separate you from your child. Be willing to file appeals and gain support from local churches, organizations and community leaders.

Scenario #4:
Because of your faith and conviction, you believe marriage is the best route to take. You have a leadership role in the church and do not want the news to get out that you fathered a child and walked away from the mother. Now you know the mother is evil and has several issues, but you ignore them and walk down the aisle. Years later the two of you separate and now all you want is a relationship with your child. The mother lets you see the child when it is convenient for her and continuously uses the relationship you have with your child

against you. She consistently degrades you in front of your child and is pretty clear about one thing–making your life a living hell!

What Do You Do?

A. Endure the drama and disrespect.
B. File for joint custody and take her to court every time she violates the order.
C. File for joint custody but do nothing when she violates the order because you don't want to see the mother of your child go to jail.
D. Fight back verbally and continue to foster a hostile environment for your child/children.
E. Just see your child on the days that she brings your child by the house–just to avoid the drama.

I normally see most men doing "E". Doing this may seem like the decision that will cause less drama, but in reality, the drama will never cease if you don't deal with the matter in the correct way. When you are not willing and able to fight for yourself, find someone who can fight on your behalf. Though you may be reluctant to take your battle to the court room, it may be the only place you can receive the judgment you deserve.

Don't be afraid to take your child's mother to court, especially if she is violating your rights as a father.

Remember, court can be avoided when you are dealing with a parent-partner who has a mature heart and the ability to effectively communicate. However, all women are not fair and sometimes getting a dose of their own medicine will suddenly bring things into perspective. If she knows that you will not take her to court, she will continue to violate your rights as a father.

It is imperative that you learn how to advocate for yourself so you can advocate for others. Men you must stand up and let your voice be heard. Volunteer with local organizations that are working to alleviate the burdens you face. Without a doubt, support the Can I Live Fatherhood Initiative.

CHAPTER SIX
Do's and Don'ts

If you are served with child support papers or threatened to be taken to child support court, here is a list of do's and don'ts. If you follow them, you will be steps closer to staying out of child support court.

DO NOT #1:

Quit your job! Quitting is the ultimate cop out and you will lose any if all respect. You lose any respect. This screams irresponsibility, immaturity, and a whole bunch of other words that I choose to not disclose... I think you get my point.

Did you know that even if you quit your job, the amount you owe for child support will continue to accrue and eventually it will come back to haunt you. The numbers of men that get arrested these days for failure to pay child support are astronomical. And guess what, if you are not a bum, you will at some point in your life have to get a job.

Working off the books may keep food in your mouth temporarily, but it will never advance your quality of life or put you in a position to properly head your household. No real man would quit their job to avoid paying child support.

DO NOT #2:

Refuse to answer the summons or tell whomever you are staying with to tell the sheriff that you do not live there! You will not escape this irresponsible decision. The person who does this is headed for trouble! Man up and do what real men do–take care of their responsibilities.

Remember I stated the parable which talked about the man who brings trouble upon his family (children are considered your family). This man inherits the wind. This could explain the reason why you have something good only for a moment. The wind blows and you know not from which direction it comes.

DO NOT #3:

Take the issues that you and your ex are going through out on the children. For example, if you made a date to see your child and the mother does something to upset you, DO NOT cancel on your children. This keeps you in hot water and justifies her taking you to court. Missing scheduled days to see your children could negatively affect your case in a custody hearing. YOU MUST separate your feelings about her from how you support your children. The children are innocent in this whole matter. You as the father owe it to them, not her, to be a responsible parent.

Despite the name-calling, try your best to ignore the disrespect. She is not angry; she is hurt. Be a good father and treat your child's mother in a manner that shows your sensitivity to her feelings and respect to her as a woman. Be strong for her and your children for they will look to you for strength.

Understand that anger is not a primary emotion but more of a secondary one. Individuals who are generally angry are only so because someone they love has hurt them. It is the pain (primary emotion) people encounter that makes them angry, bitter or jealous. Being emotionally mature will help you to work constructively with hurt people. Don't allow their hurt and anger to spread to you. Always be positive and supportive. Hurt people are ticking time bombs. Try to defuse the bomb before it explodes.

DO NOT #4:
Threaten to stop seeing the children once you receive child support papers. This is so juvenile and exposes your true character. If you are faced with these thoughts, REPENT. Ask GOD to remove everything within you that is not of Him. He can do it for there is nothing that is too hard for God[5].

---

5 Jeremiah 32:17 The Holy Bible.

In order to behave above your own pain, you will need to rely on something much greater than yourself. The concept of being the bigger person that I am sharing with you is in total contradiction to your natural instincts. You will have to change your heart to want to be more empathetic and supportive. Then, you must think and be smart. Making wise decisions out of love will help you avoid becoming a victim of the child support system, and worse–a dead beat dad.

DO NOT #5:
Tell the children to call Child Protective Services, or Child Welfare because the mother chooses to reprimand the children for doing something wrong. Children need discipline. Do not involve your child in some juvenile vendetta that you have against your child's mother.

DO NOT #6:
Do not use religion as a divisive mechanism to create conflict or pit your children against their mother. We talked about vindictive women, but men can be vindictive as well. Take raising your child seriously. Involving your child in the conflict between you and your parent-partner can severely harm their development.

DO NOT #7:

Become seriously involved with another woman without being open and honest to your parent-partner and considering how this relationship will affect your child.

Though you have every right to move on, it will go a long way toward developing your parent-partner relationship if you are open about your love life. This will let your parent-partner know that although you have moved on, you still respect the relationship that the two of you have. She will appreciate your honesty greatly, and it may help to relieve feelings of hurt or confusion that she may be harboring.

Also, you should respect your child's youthful inability to understand adult relationships. Be open and honest with your child, but protect them from over-exposure to your new relationships. If you are dating, be careful who you introduce and expose to your children. If you are dating several women, do not parade them in front of your child. Be sure that anyone you introduce to your child is not some passing flame.

DO NOT #8:

Allow your significant other to pick up your children, babysit, or have access to your child without the consent of your parent-partner. It is your shared duty as parents to protect the safety and well- being of your child. Allowing someone to have access to your child without the consent of the mother is reckless and irresponsible. If she does not consent, make arrangements for childcare that do not include your significant other. This is only fair as you would ask the same of her. Remember, being a good parent-partner is about open communication and reciprocity. Show her the same respect that you demand. Allowing access to your child without consent can be a strike against you and could mean child support court.

DO NOT #9:

Involve your child in adult affairs, particularly in regards to matters that may be too advanced for them to understand. Children have difficulty dealing with relationships, sex, and separations. Be sensitive about needlessly exposing your children to matters that may scar them or cause traumatic stress. There will be times that you have to discuss these topics with your children, but be deliberate in protecting them from harm as much as possible. Remember, they are not adults. The children don't care and this will only complicate matters for them. The only thing they want is to have both a mother and a father. If having the both of you means arguing, fighting, and drama on top of drama then they are better off without the two of you being together.

DO NOT #10:

Move out of state without communicating that fact with your parent-partner. If you move without letting your parent-partner know, she may get the impression that you are trying to run from your responsibilities. This is all a part of maintaining an open, honest relationship. Men, soon as women hear you are leaving or considering moving out of state; it is her lack of trust for you that will prompt her to take you to child support court.

DO NOT #11:

After taking care of all of her children (you and her together as a family unit) decide after a break-up that you will now only be a part of your children or child's life. If you have been supporting the other children that are not yours financially, emotionally and physically; terminating the relationship with the children that are not yours magnifies the cracks in your character. Although you may not be able to financially afford to pay for them all; try your best and make sure the children never sense a breach in the bond that you once had. The woman's pain is her children's pain. When you bring pain to the children, rest assured that she will attempt to bring pain to you. Although she may not want to admit it; if she takes you to child support court, it is likely because she believes in her heart that you maliciously intended to hurt her children. She will feel justified and vindicated by taking you to court.

Don't let yourself be in a place like this. The decision might seem difficult, but when your heart is mature and strong, it is very easy! Be considerate of your stepchildren's feelings (regardless of your marital status). Children are young and vulnerable in these situations. They will need your continued love and support.

DO #1:
Separate how you feel about her and your feelings for your children. You may not like her, but you love your children, or at least you should. This will take some time. Try to avoid phone contact for at least one week after you receive child support papers. This gives you time to calm down, think, and act logically in developing a strategy to approach the child support system and your child's mother. Focus on your children and be strong for them.

Chapter Six: Do's and Don'ts

The more you focus on the love that you have for your children, the more you will begin to realize that they are the most important components of your life and how you deal with them will make an imprint on the type of person they will grow up to be.

DO #2:

If you are still angry after one week write her a letter. Women respond well to letters. Refrain from fowl words and negative connotations. Write her a letter explaining how you do not like how things have become unproductive and you would like to sit down and speak to her about HOW YOU CAN HELP HER raise your child/children. The last thing you want her to do is be a single mother and to have your child grow up without a strong relationship with his or her father.

It is rarely about the money, but more about the relationship with your children. I have heard more women say that they would give back every dime of child support if only the dad would be a FATHER to their child. I put that word in all caps because it is that important. It means everything.

DO #3:

Offer to maintain the lawn (cut the grass), clean out the garage, or fix something that is broken around the house for your parent-partner if at all possible. This keeps her from having to do it herself or hire someone to do it for her. This will score major points! Obviously there are some situations that can make this act of support complicated. If you are in a relationship, this may be something that your significant other may consent to or adamantly oppose. Be sure that you don't make matters worse by simply trying to be helpful. You know your situation. If you can help without creating a mess of the situation, do so.

However, if going to your parent-partner's home to help her maintain her house is going to cause more problems than it solves, find other ways to be helpful. Remember, helping her around the house should be a strictly plutonic act of support for your parent-partner as you try to help maintain a clean, safe, healthy environment for your child and parent-partner. She may absolutely get mixed signals and may be turned on by your ability to man up. Women are attracted to strength; such strength should be displayed as discipline.

Chapter Six: Do's and Don'ts

In other words, if your parent-partner comes down the stairs wearing something irresistibly enticing- what do you do? D.I.G. and FLEE! It is a trap! Crossing the lines at this point will definitely backfire and prove unfavorable for you in the end. Yes, she will be upset that you rejected her but eventually she will respect the level you have raised your "A" game. Yes, she may try to come at you another way, especially if she is not over the relationship. If you know this to be true then this technique will not work for you. These tips are for grown and mature individuals. If you are not good with fixing things around the house, please don't try–find someone who is and pay them.

You will have to communicate with her that although she is a beautiful woman that part of your relationship is over. If you are unable to resist her, she will be able to play that card at various times only to her convenience. Most men will fail that part of the test. Just know that if you continue to be intimate with your parent-partner and you have no intentions of making her your wife, it will only keep emotions high at a time when you are working to control them.

DO #4:
Take your boy(s) to get haircuts or cut it yourself, and make yourself frequently available to help with situations like this. If you have girls,

take them to a salon to have their hair professionally done. In addition to making sure your children are well-groomed, pay attention to these small tasks that are huge burdens on single mothers who are already overburdened. Showing support in these type tasks not only mean the world to your parent-partner, it will also mean the world to your child.

It cannot be overstated how difficult it is to be a single mother. Be there for your parent-partner and raising your children will be made much easier. It will also make a major difference in the growth and development of your child.

DO #5:
Drop off small thank you cards in the mailbox. This thank you card should emphasize what a wonderful job she is doing as a mother. Mention the fact that you guys work great as a parenting team and you appreciate all that she does in keeping the children well groomed, well behaved and on the right track.

All women want is to feel appreciated, respected, and not taken for granted. If you knew what her daily grind as a mother entailed, you would give her credit because chances are she really deserves it.

Chapter Six: Do's and Don'ts

If you acknowledge and show appreciation for her hard work from the heart, you will win her faithful cooperative partnership in raising

DO #6:
Treat the mother of your children to an hour or more at a spa or similar service where she can get away from the children (on holidays, birthdays and special events if your income allows for it). You do not have to wait until Mother's Day to give your parent-partner a gift. Show her that you appreciate her hard work. A spa treatment is a great idea for a gift. After receiving such a thoughtful gift, your parent-partner will be calling her friends to tell them what a great parent-partner you are.

Nothing builds teamwork like saying "thank you" for a job well done. Whether it's a spa treatment or picking up the kids on your off days, you will have her calling everyone she knows to tell them how blessed she is to have a man like you as the father of her children.

DO #7:
Maintain a consistent track record of picking up your children. If you say that you are going to be there at a certain time and place, be there

as if it were your job. You need to become so dependable when it comes to the children, that when all else fails, she is confident of one thing, you will be there for your children!

There is nothing worse than having the children await your visit and you never show up. Can we say DISASTER! The children are left devastated by your no show and your parent-partner will have to alter her plans. This is irresponsible and could affect your case in a custody hearing. Be dependable and keep scheduled visits with your child/children.

DO #8:
Offer to take the children if she decides to go back to school. Whether it is in the evening, or on weekends, offering to take the children while she continues her education is HUGE! She will not know what to do with you. One thing is guaranteed, child support is the farthest thing from her mind.

Helping your parent-partner work to advance her education is an investment in your child's quality of life and development. As a supportive father, your parent-partner will have no reason to sue you for child support. With all that you do to support her, she will be afraid to lose some of the nice things that you do for her as a result of child support court demands. Defusing the time-bomb inside of your child's mother requires you to be proactive. The better you treat her the more the bomb is dismantled. The more you ignore her needs and feelings, the louder the bomb will tick until it finally EXPLODES.

DO #9:
Coach a local football, basketball, baseball, or soccer league for some of the kids in the neighborhood. This way if you have boys, they can play for free. If you have girls, volunteering with their girl scouts troop, or taking her to dance will give you the quality time you need to build her self-esteem. This type of initiative speaks volumes in attesting to your character.

Character will take you places money cannot! Money did not make Martin Luther King great. It was his character. Character is who you are at your core and what you do when no one is looking. Having good character as a father means being supportive, honest, caring, and dependable.

After having children, your primary responsibility is to recognize their natural gifts and train them up in the way that leads them to their divine purpose. Parenting is more than simply providing monetary and tangible benefits. It is preparing and equipping them with every tool available so that they are able to increase what it is you have built and established in the earth. The focus shifts from yourself to your offspring. This can be difficult as it requires a re-posturing or re-positioning of your heart.

No one is suggesting that you change instantly if you are not already doing the things that I have suggested thus far. You will need practice to develop your ability to communicate past pain and do the things that will foster a strong parent-partner relationship. Understand that it will take time, commitment, and hard work, but once you decide in your heart to be a better father and parent-partner it is just a matter of time before your goals become a reality. Though change won't happen instantly, there is no better time to start than right here, right now!

If you have moved on and are currently in a relationship with someone else and she begins to take offense to your efforts to be a better father, then you might want to reconsider this new relationship. Any woman who attempts to come between you and your role as a father and parent-partner likely has issues that will prove problematic for you in the long run. A good mate will support your efforts to be a good father and parent-partner, as long as your character warrants such sacrifice.

CHAPTER SEVEN
The Game Plan

Okay, you have read through the entire book. We have covered the nature of relationships, the wiring of a woman, what happens when you are caught up, what to do when you are in a Catch 22, and most importantly the "Do's" and "Don'ts" of fatherhood. The tips covered in the previous chapters should be incorporated in your new life, relationship and way of thinking. The techniques discussed don't go well with fool's play. What do I mean, when I say fool's play? Fool's play is not taking relationships seriously, not being empathetic in regards to the feeling of others, not being there for your children, and hurting the people that love you and vice versa. It won't be easy but the benefits of being a good man and father are everlasting.

If your mind-set has shifted somewhat after reading this book, then it is your duty to spread what you've learned. Fatherhood is at a critical low. Do your part in building stronger families and thus better communities. The purpose of this book is to start conversations among men that lead to an increase in paternal involvement in the lives of our youth.

As mentioned earlier there is no cookie cutter game plan, whereas one size fits all. What we will do in this chapter is cover the basics of what every game plan needs to have. Every Game Plan must be built on:

A Vision:

Without a vision you will be bound to doing the things of your past. You need something that will push you to keep moving. Vision is something you see internally that compels and drives you to make it a reality. What do you want to be in life? What is your purpose? Write down a two-column description that highlights the current life you have (emotionally, financially, mentally, and physically) in one column, and in the other column the life you want and desire (no matter how crazy and far-fetched you may think it is, write it down anyway).

Look at where you are and where you want to be. This understanding is the first step in your journey. Knowledge is half the battle to progress. Hard work and better decision-making will carry you to the finish line.

As you plan your future, start by setting goals. After you establish your long-term and short-term goals, answer the following questions to help you develop details of your plan.

Write down your answers!

1. Is this goal within my reach? Is it realistic?
2. Who do I need to assist me with accomplishing this goal?
3. What resources does this goal require me to have? (i.e. money, education, support, knowledge, training, or expertise from outsiders)
4. Where will I get the resources from?
5. How will I know if I am on track?
6. Why is this goal significant to my life?
7. What are the benefits of accomplishing this goal?

Having a Game Plan helps you stay on track and be able to identify when and where you get off course in life. It will ultimately serve as a guide and roadmap that will take you from where you are to where you want to be. Your Game Plan is your personal GPS system. A good plan will direct you to manifesting your dreams. It will also get you back on track if you ever were to lose your way.

Chapter Seven: The Game Plan

Identify who you will need to help you with accomplishing the steps in your Game Plan. If you cannot find any friends and or family members to help, there are many non-profits that offer free workshops on goal setting and life skill development. There are professionals who would love to mentor you and help you achieve your goals.

The keys to executing your Game Plan successfully are planning, preparation, practice, practice and more practice. You must make your Game Plan a part of your everyday walk and talk in life. In time, you will become the exemplary father and parent-partner. If necessary, read the book over and over until you see yourself doing the things that are written in this book. To further clarify, let's take a look at how we earn points in the Game Plan.

First Point in the Game Plan:
Stop having kids out of wedlock that you cannot afford. That is number one. In order to stop having kids, you will have to do one of the following: Stop having sex or begin using protection.

Having sex without a condom is dangerous. You should never have sex without protection. Abstinence is even safer, and the best choice for birth control if you are not married. This, I understand, is easier said than done.

Second Point in the Game Plan:

Enroll in school. That's right I said school. Some of us have become so lazy in our thinking that school has become what kryptonite was to Superman. The question you must ask yourself is, "Where and how far will my current skills take me in today's job market?" A man that will does not work, does not eat[6]. If you cannot work, you will not eat. Who does not want to eat? Only the man that wishes to perish and die. A man that cannot provide does not feel like a man, for this is your primary responsibility as a man. If you are reading this book, I believe that this is not you. You want to work, you want to provide and take care of your children. You have dreams that you would like to see come true one day. You are NOT the trifling lazy dead beat dad that cares only about himself. If you are, decide that you will no longer feed that stereotype. Repent, turn around and go the other way.

People perish simply because of the lack of knowledge. Knowledge is one thing that we have an abundance of in our society today. Your

---

6 II Thessalonians 3:10 The Holy Bible

unwillingness to obtain it will cause you and everyone depending on you to perish. Is this how God wants it? Absolutely Not! Enroll in the academic or vocational training that is right for you and make learning a lifelong pursuit. Increasing your knowledge and earning power enables you to adequately support yourself and family.

Third Point in the Game Plan:
Enroll in school. And yes, I just said that. It is so vital and an absolute that you have to hear it again from a different perspective. Today's job market will require academic degrees or skills that can only be acquired through specialized training. As manufacturing jobs move overseas, the future of the job market in the U.S. will be in skilled jobs. Technology is changing the way companies are doing business. It allows businesses to lower their cost and lower their risk. Technology is threaded and infused in every part of our lives just as public policy is. The skills that are demanded in today's job market are becoming more complex and requiring highly specialized skills and abilities. I don't think I can stress enough that education is knowledge and knowledge is power. For you to acquire the skills that make you attractive to a company, it is imperative that you acquire skills based training or academic degrees specific to the needs of the position you are seeking. Doing this will qualify you for the jobs you seek and

the jobs that are seeking you. Financial aid in the form of student loans helps reduce the stress associated with school. Be smart, use refunds wisely and be the number one investor in your future.

Fourth Point in the Game Plan:

D.I.G., D.I.G., and keep D.I.G.'ing. Delay Instant Gratification! The key to preventing many of the problems that you will ever face in life lies within this simple, yet challenging concept. We are challenged by our temptations, but His help enables you to use discipline. God encourages our hearts to deny ourselves the sinful and unhealthy pleasures in life that only serve to harm us physically, mentally, and spiritually. Be strong. Follow your heart. Say "no" to unprotected sex. Say "no" to unwanted pregnancy. Say "no" to everything negative thought and deed that presents itself as a distraction to your plan of action.

This Game plan is simple and easy to follow. It is my hope that you take the lessons from this book and prepare your heart to be a great father and parent-partner. The system will victimize you if you have not done your due diligence in supporting your child, fostering a good relationship with your parent partner, or working to earn a living that will provide sustenance to you and your family.

Chapter Seven: The Game Plan

I hope I wasn't too hard on you brothers but we are on a hard and rough journey. It's difficult to think that many of our struggles come from our own ignorant decisions. If you are reading this and you think of someone else who would benefit from reading this book, tell them about what you have learned and suggest that they pick up a copy.

I am committed to help strengthen families by encouraging males to live healthy lives, be better fathers, work to be better parent-partners, and furthermore encourage other men to do the same. I am also committed to the same mission for women. ***Get Your Hands Off My Butt: The Hands-On Guide to Avoiding the Welfare System*** encourages females to live healthy, virtuous lives and become better women and parent-partners.

Keep up with the Hands-On Tour and other products offered by following me on **Instagram @the.brillionaire**.

Fight the good fight of faith with the right weapons. You can look to us for an arsenal of resources that will help you do just that.

Until next time.

ACKNOWLEDGEMENT
A Father Forever...

Fathers Forever is a non-profit organization that serves as a map to help fathers chart a new course of fatherhood through a 24 week 30-hour curriculum and support group. The purpose of Fathers Forever is to increase the number of fathers who support their children, decrease the number of men imprisoned for child support cases and commit resources that will motivate, educate, and equip men to become better fathers and co-parents in their children's lives.

As a single parent who has raised three children to adulthood, Glenwood L. Warren, Founder and Executive Director of Fathers Forever (**www.afatherforever.com**) understands the power and necessity of fathers being a contributing, positive presence in the lives of their children. While prison punishes, it does nothing to help men who simply need help. According to Fathers Forever, a recent Men Against Domestic Violence survey indicated that:

- 85% of all children who exhibit behavioral disorders come from fatherless homes.

- 71% of all high school dropouts come from fatherless homes.
- 75% of all adolescent patients in chemical abuse centers come from fatherless homes.
- 70% of juveniles in state operated institutions come from fatherless homes.
- 85% of all youth sitting in prisons grew up in fatherless homes.
- 80% of rapists motivated with displaced anger come from fatherless homes.
- 90% of all homeless and runaway children are from fatherless homes.

Fathers Forever's goal is to decrease the number of children being raised without the support of their fathers. Since receiving its first participant in April of 2010, over 170 men have successfully completed the Fathers Forever 24-week program and 80% of them have graduated with jobs and increased their child-support obligations.

Support the *Fathers'* Initiative

Improving child support laws will make a tremendous difference in terms of the number of men who are wrongly jailed and the number of children adversely affected by these laws. We believe that it is absolutely critical that we protect the rights of poor men and work to make sure that our laws work for the good of man in the spirit that they were created.

CaniLive
Bringing Opportunity Home
www.canilive.org

Got Child Support Insurance?

Visit
www.progenylife.com

PROGENY LIFE

CHILD SUPPORT INSURANCE PROTECTION

Securing Your Children's Future Today!

(800) 636-9953

@leopolemclaughlin

Racquel Williams-Jones

Author of the Hands-On book collection which includes, Get Your Hands Out My Pocket: The Hands-On Guide to Avoiding the Child Support System; and Get Your Hands Off My Butt: The Hands-On Guide to Avoiding the Welfare System uses her personal challenges and triumphs to advance leadership and personal development capacity, creative self-sufficiency pathways and systems navigation.

Her vision will move you beyond chaotic relationships, poor communication which leads to distractors outcomes and unmoving financial gains.

Can I Live
Bringing Opportunity Home
www.canilive.org

Visit Our website to learn more about products and services offered by Can I Live, Inc.

Made in the USA
Middletown, DE
23 June 2023